T0001635

VEGAN SNACKS

VEGAN SNACKS

Over 60 recipes for tasty plant-based bites

LONDON • NEW YORK

Designer Geoff Borin
Senior Editor Abi Waters
Head of Production Patricia Harrington
Editorial Director Julia Charles
Creative Director Leslie Harrington
Indexer Vanessa Bird

First published in 2024
by Ryland Peters & Small
20–21 Jockey's Fields
London WC1R 4BW and
341 E 116th Street, New York, 10029

www.rylandpeters.com

10 9 8 7 6 5 4 3 2 1

Text copyright © Caroline Artiss,
Ross Dobson, Ursula Ferrigno, Nicola
Graimes, Dunja Gulin, Vicky Jones,
Jackie Kearney, Anya Ladra, Hannah
Miles, Louise Pickford, Leah Vandervelft,
Laura Washburn Hutton, Jenna Zoe
and Ryland Peters & Small 2024
(see also page 128 for full credits)
Design and photographs copyright ©
Ryland Peters & Small 2024

ISBN: 978-1-78879-579-1

A CIP record for this book is available
from the British Library.

US Library of Congress CIP data has
been applied for.

Printed in China

Notes

• Both British (Metric) and American
(Imperial and US cups) measurements
are included in these recipes for your
convenience, however it is important to
work with one set of measurements and
not alternate between the two.

• Buy unwaxed citrus fruit and wash
before zesting. If you can only find treated
fruit, scrub well before using.

• Always check the product packaging to
ensure the particular brand of ingredient
you are buying is vegan.

MIX
Paper | Supporting
responsible forestry
FSC® C008047
www.fsc.org

Contents

Introduction

Snacks are the mood-boosting, energy-bolstering treats that everyone looks forward to. What's an enjoyable weekend without a bowl or platter of indulgent munchies to share? Or a good gym session without a nutritious snack to re-fuel afterwards? They really are essential pick-me-ups at any time of day, from a few bites with mid-morning coffee to an afternoon morsel when energy is flagging.

Evidence has shown that munching in between meals is a healthy habit, but only when the food is unprocessed and full of good, nourishing ingredients. With this book of over 60 plant-based recipes, you can quit processed convenience snacks full of salt, sugar and dairy and choose a healthier way to graze that looks out for your well-being and the well-being of the planet, too. Once you have your favourite recipes down, try making big batches at the start of the week, ready to grab and go when hunger strikes.

Start your day off the right way with some vegan-friendly breakfast options, such as The Ultimate Breakfast Sandwich or a Savoury Granola Bar. The On-the-go chapter features convenient and portable recipes perfect for an active lifestyle. Try packing super-healthy Himalayan Energy Bars in your bag before a hike. Or whip up a batch of Chocolate & Avocado balls, they taste like truffles but are full of healthy fats and nutrients! Sample savoury recipes from the Grazing chapter such as the ridiculously moreish Thai Green Curry Popcorn or Spicy Tomato Kale Chips that use plenty of herbs and spices to bring out the delicious flavours of the natural produce. Get busy with the selection of easy recipes for Bar Bites, perfect for enjoying with a drink, from Gourd and Cashew Koftas to Jalapeño Onion Rings. Finally, Sweet Treats is a sweet-toothed vegan's dream come true – from Coffee Cookies and Chocolate Banana Bread to Coconut and Cherry Drops, these delightful bites are bound to hit the spot.

Whatever your reasons for avoiding animal products, whether ethical, environmental, health-benefits or a mixture of all three, you'll find a whole host of recipes here that will revolutionize your snacking and munching. Satisfy bad cravings with this virtuous food, which proves once and for all that plant-based snacking can be every bit as delicious as it is good for you!

Chapter 1

DAYBREAK

Sunrise snacks to start the day

Green smoothie bowl

This is a refreshing yet rich, creamy smoothie bowl – perfect for a hot summer morning.

120 ml/½ cup almond milk

220 g/1½ cups frozen spinach

1 frozen banana, broken into pieces

75 g/½ cup frozen mango chunks

1–2 tablespoons smooth peanut butter

OPTIONAL ADD-INS
1 teaspoon coconut oil

1 tablespoon flaxseeds

1 tablespoon chia seeds

OPTIONAL TOPPINGS
granola

cacao nibs

coconut flakes

extra peanut butter

fresh fruit

SERVES 1

Pour the almond milk into the base of a blender. Add the spinach, banana and mango and start to blend at high speed. As the mixture is blending, pause once or twice to scrape down the sides with a rubber spatula to make sure that everything is well incorporated.

When the mixture is smooth, stop the blender, then add the peanut butter and any optional add-ins.

Blend again until everything is smooth and thick. Pour the smoothie into a bowl to serve and finish with your chosen toppings.

Breakfast smoothie

This delicious drink will definitely help to sustain your energy levels until lunchtime.

1 banana

1 small mango

125 g/1 cup blueberries

50 g/⅓ cup muesli

500 ml/2 cups apple juice

MAKES 3 DRINKS

Peel and chop the banana. To prepare the mango, slice down each side of the pit/stone and cut away the flesh from the skin. Put the banana and mango in a blender with the blueberries, muesli and apple juice. Blend until smooth. Pour into glasses and serve immediately.

Date & banana frappé

Dates provide a quick energy boost, satisfy sugar cravings and give the shake a delicious caramel flavour.

4 Medjool dates, pitted/stoned

125 ml/½ cup apple juice

2 bananas

300 ml/1¼ cups rice milk

MAKES 2 DRINKS

Put the dates and apple juice in a small saucepan, heat gently until boiling, then cover and simmer for 5 minutes until the dates have softened. Let cool completely. Transfer the dates and juice to a blender. Peel and chop the bananas, add them and the rice milk to the blender and blend until smooth. Pour into glasses and serve immediately.

Creamy berry soy shake

This is a thick and totally delicious fruit drink. You could substitute berry sorbet for the soy ice cream for a change.

125 g/1 cup raspberries

100 g/¾ cup blackberries

2 scoops vanilla soy ice cream

500 ml/2 cups soy milk

MAKES 2–3 DRINKS

Put all the ingredients together in a blender and blend until smooth. Pour into glasses and serve immediately.

Soy & tahini smoothie

Tahini helps to boost calcium levels and also creates a deliciously creamy smoothie.

1 banana

2 tablespoons tahini

2 tablespoons maple syrup

300 ml/1¼ cups soy milk

250 ml/1 cup soy yogurt

MAKES 2 DRINKS

Peel the banana, chop the flesh and put in a blender with the remaining ingredients. Blend until smooth. Pour into glasses and serve immediately.

Topped toasts

Try out these suggestions for both sweet and savoury toast toppings or get creative and experiment with different combinations of ingredients to make the perfect breakfast.

Sweet toppings (SERVES 1)

PEANUT BUTTER & BERRY

2 slices of bread

2 tablespoons peanut butter

50–60 g/⅓–½ cup fresh berries or thawed frozen berries

honey, to serve

hemp seeds, to serve

Toast the bread to your desired toastiness. Slather on peanut butter. Top with berries, a drizzle of honey and a sprinkle of hemp seeds.

BANANA & SEED

2 slices of bread

2 tablespoons almond butter

1 banana, sliced into rounds

½ teaspoon hemp seeds

½ teaspoon chia seeds

1 teaspoon pumpkin seeds/pepitas

Toast the bread to your desired toastiness. Spread with a generous amount of almond butter. Top with banana slices and sprinkle on the seeds.

HAZELNUT CHOC SPREAD

130 g/1 cup hazelnuts

2 tablespoons melted coconut oil

2 tablespoons maple syrup or honey

2 tablespoons cocoa powder

1 teaspoon vanilla extract

pinch of sea salt

2 slices of bread

sliced strawberries, to serve

toasted hazelnuts, roughly chopped, to serve

Preheat the oven to 180°C (350°F) Gas 4.

Spread the hazelnuts out on a dry baking sheet. Pop in the preheated oven for 5 minutes, shake the tray and return to the oven for another 5 minutes until lightly toasted. If the skins are on the hazelnuts, cover the baking tray with a kitchen towel and allow to cool for about 5–10 minutes.

Remove the skins by rolling your hands over the towel covering the nuts. You're trying to jostle them enough so the skins begin to fall away. Getting about three quarters off is a win here, some are very stubborn. Transfer to a food processor or high speed blender and process for about 5–8 minutes. Push beyond the fine powder until you get a denser, softened nut butter.

Add the melted coconut oil, syrup or honey, cocoa powder, vanilla and sea salt and blend for 1–2 minutes until smooth.

Toast the bread, slather on the chocolate spread and top with sliced strawberries and chopped toasted hazelnuts.

Savoury toppings

ROASTED CARROT & HUMMUS

4 carrots

a splash of olive oil, plus extra for drizzling

2 slices of bread

1 garlic clove, cut in half

60 g/¼ cup hummus

2–4 teaspoons dukkah

2 teaspoons freshly chopped parsley

sea salt and freshly ground black pepper

SERVES 1

Preheat the oven to 220°C (425°F) Gas 7.

Peel and roughly chop the carrots and toss with the oil and a big pinch of salt. Place on a baking sheet and roast in the oven for 25–30 minutes until golden and brown at the edges.

Toast the bread to your liking. Rub the warm bread with the cut sides of the garlic clove.

Spread the bread with hummus and top with roasted carrots, dukkah and parsley. Drizzle with olive oil and season with salt and pepper.

PEAS & SPINACH

olive oil for frying, plus extra for serving

1 garlic clove, finely chopped

125 g/1 cup frozen peas, thawed

large handful of baby spinach

1 teaspoon lemon juice, plus extra to taste

2 large slices (or 4 small) of sourdough

1 garlic clove, cut in half

sea salt and freshly ground black pepper

goat's cheese or capers (optional), to serve

SERVES 2

In a medium frying pan/skillet, heat a thin layer of oil over a medium heat. Add the garlic and stir-fry for 20–30 seconds before adding the peas and spinach. Cook, stirring regularly, for about 3 minutes until everything is warmed through and the spinach has wilted. Season with salt and lemon juice and remove from the heat.

Mash the pan contents lightly with a fork or potato masher, or pulse everything in a food processor or blender. You're looking for a texture that is somewhere between a smooth purée and completely whole, so that the peas can stay atop the toast without rolling off.

Meanwhile, toast the bread to your desired toastiness. Rub the warm bread with the cut sides of the garlic clove.

Spread the pea mixture on the toast. Top with goat's cheese and/or capers, if using, and some black pepper.

Note: I love adding a little salty garnish like capers, goat's cheese or feta to offset the natural sweetness of the peas, but just a small sprinkle of sea salt can help you with that, too.

Ultimate breakfast sandwich

This breakfast sandwich has got creamy elements and enough tang from harissa and barbecue sauce to keep it interesting.

1 butternut squash, peeled

1 avocado, peeled and pitted/stoned

1 tablespoon freshly chopped coriander/cilantro (optional)

4 English muffins

sea salt

barbecue sauce, to serve

TAHINI-HARISSA DRESSING

50 g/¼ cup tahini

1 garlic clove, peeled

1 teaspoon harissa paste

½ teaspoon sea salt

1 tablespoon fresh lemon juice

SERVES 4

Preheat the oven to 200°C (400°F) Gas 6. Slice the neck or handle part of the butternut squash into 1.5-cm/½-inch thick rounds (save the hollowed-out base of the squash for another recipe). Spread the rounds out on an oiled baking sheet and season with salt to taste. Roast for 30 minutes, turning halfway, until tender.

Make the dressing by blending all the ingredients in a food processor or blender with 60 ml/¼ cup water until smooth.

Lightly mash the avocado with a pinch of salt and the chopped coriander, if using.

When you're ready to serve, split and toast the English muffins. Spread the tahini-harissa dressing on one half of each, top with a butternut round or two and drizzle with barbecue sauce.

Spread the mashed avocado on the other half of each muffin and sandwich everything together.

Chickpea socca pancakes

These versatile vegan pancakes also work with roasted tomatoes or coconut yogurt and sliced fruit.

125 g/1 cup chickpea/gram flour

½ teaspoon salt

olive oil, for frying

grated vegan Parmesan, for topping (optional)

FOR THE MUSHROOMS

1 tablespoon olive oil

5 sprigs of fresh thyme, leaves removed from the stems

225 g/8 oz. cremini mushrooms, sliced

1 garlic clove, grated

sea salt and freshly ground black pepper

SERVES 2

Put the chickpea flour, salt and 295 ml/1¼ cups water into a large bowl and mix together with a whisk or a fork into a smooth batter. Leave to stand at room temperature for at least 10 minutes.

Meanwhile, for the mushrooms, heat a thin layer of oil in a frying pan/skillet over a high heat. Add the thyme and mushrooms and cook, stirring often, for 2–3 minutes until the mushrooms are slightly golden. Reduce the heat to medium, then add the garlic and cook for 1 minute more. Season to taste with salt and pepper. Keep the mushrooms warm in a low oven or in a covered dish while you cook the pancakes.

Heat the olive oil in another small frying pan/skillet over a medium heat. Add about 60 ml/ ¼ cup of the socca batter to the pan. Swirl it around so that it covers the base of the pan. Fry for about 2–3 minutes, until the batter begins to form bubbles, flip, then cook for 1–2 minutes on the other side. Repeat with the remaining batter. Serve with the mushrooms and any additional toppings you like.

Ginger & cashew granola bars

If you're one of those people who is always working around a busy schedule, you'll be thankful for this recipe! Because the granola is pre-made, these tasty no-bake bars just require assembly and patience while they set.

200 g/1¾ cups plain granola

60 g/½ cup well-chopped cashews

40 g/¼ cup well-chopped crystallized ginger

80 g/1 cup crisped rice cereal

50 g/¼ cup almond butter

115 g/⅓ cup brown rice syrup

1 tablespoon vegetable oil

20-cm/8-in square baking pan, greased and lined with baking parchment

MAKES 12

Mix the granola, cashews, ginger and crisped rice cereal together in a large mixing bowl. Add the almond butter, rice syrup and oil and mix well so everything is well-coated.

Press the sticky batter into the pan and set in the fridge to set for at least 3 hours.

Remove from the fridge and cut into even bars before serving.

Variation: Candied citrus peel is a great option instead of crystallized ginger in this recipe and gives the bars a tropical burst of tangy citrus.

Savoury breakfast bars

These no-bake granola bars will provide enough energy to keep you going on a busy day.

60 g/½ cup walnuts, toasted and chopped

55 g/⅓ cup pumpkin seeds/ pepitas, toasted

55 g/⅓ cup sesame seeds, toasted

90 g/1 cup jumbo rolled oats

40 g/1 cup wholegrain unsweetened puffed rice

10 g/¼ oz. kale chips, torn into small pieces

1 teaspoon hot smoked paprika

2 tablespoons coconut oil

175 g/¾ cup brown rice syrup

3 tablespoons almond butter

sea salt, to taste

25 x 20-cm/10 x 8-inch baking pan, lined with clingfilm/plastic wrap, leaving some overhanging

MAKES 15

Place the walnuts, seeds, oats, puffed rice, kale chips and smoked paprika in a mixing bowl. Season with a little salt to taste, and stir well until everything is combined.

Gently heat the coconut oil and rice syrup in a pan until melted. Remove from the heat and stir in the almond butter. Pour into the dry ingredients and mix well.

Tip the puffed rice mixture into the prepared baking pan and spread out into an even layer with the back of a wet spoon, pressing it down firmly. Fold over the cling film/plastic wrap to cover the top of the mixture, then chill for 1 hour to firm up.

Cut into 15 bars. Keep stored in the fridge in an airtight container for up to 1 week.

Chapter 2

ON-THE-GO

Balls, bars and bites for busy days

Chocolate & avocado balls

It's hard to tell these creamy, decadent balls of goodness are totally vegan and full of nutrients.

280 g/10 oz. vegan dark/bittersweet chocolate (70% cocoa solids)

1 tablespoon agave syrup or caster/granulated sugar

1 ripe avocado, halved

pinch of sea salt

½ teaspoon vanilla extract

POSSIBLE COATINGS (choose one or a mixture)

desiccated/shredded coconut

chopped pistachios

chopped flaked/slivered almonds

chopped hazelnuts

cocoa powder

MAKES 20

Break the chocolate into small pieces and pop into a heatproof bowl. Set the bowl over a pan of barely simmering water and stir to melt. Once melted, stir in the agave syrup or sugar. Set aside to cool slightly.

Scoop the avocado flesh into a large mixing bowl, discarding the stone. Add the salt and mash it to a very fine pulp.

Add the avocado to the cooled melted chocolate with the vanilla and gently fold together. Pop the mixture in the fridge to set for 30 minutes, or until much more firm.

Meanwhile, put the coatings in shallow bowls.

Next, roll the chocolate mixture into balls. Scoop a small tablespoon into the palms of your hands and quickly roll it into a ball, then immediately roll in whichever coating you want. Continue until you have used up all the chocolate mixture.

Put the balls in an airtight container and chill for at least 30 minutes before serving. Store in the fridge and eat within 2 days.

Very cherry balls

Sweet, pretty, easy to pack and nutritious, these little balls are essentially just fruit and nuts turned into small treats. They make you feel like you're eating something special!

4–6 dates, pitted/stoned

50 g/⅓ cup dried cherries

225 g/¾ cup ground hazelnuts

1 tablespoon ground flaxseeds

ground cinnamon, to taste

Bourbon vanilla powder, to taste

a little raw almond milk, if needed

coconut flour, cocoa powder or coarsely ground nuts, for coating

MAKES 15–20

Put the dates and cherries in a bowl, cover with warm water and allow to soak for 20 minutes or until soft. Drain the dates and cherries and reserve the soaking water.

Put the soaked dates and cherries in a food processor or blender and blitz until blended into a thick paste, adding a little of the reserved soaking water, if needed.

Mix together the ground nuts and seeds and add cinnamon and vanilla powder to taste. Add the puréed fruit and mix well to get a smooth, thick paste. Add a little milk if the mixture is too dry.

Take portions of the mixture about the size of chocolate truffles and roll into balls with your hands. Roll them in any (or all) of the suggested coatings. Transfer to the fridge to chill for at least 1 hour before serving.

Coconut & spirulina balls

These gloriously good-for-you energy balls are an easy and delicious way to get a daily superfood dose.

90 g/½ cup dates, pitted/stoned

65 g/½ cup cashews

1 large teaspoon coconut oil

1½–2 teaspoons spirulina powder

1 large teaspoon matcha powder (green tea powder)

about 20 g/¼ cup unsweetened desiccated coconut

MAKES 16

Soak the dates in a bowl of water for 30 minutes, but no longer than that.

Put the cashews in a food processor or blender and pulse for about 30–45 seconds until a thick meal has formed.

Rinse the dates, wipe off any extra moisture and add them to the food processor or blender along with the coconut oil, spirulina and matcha powder. Process until a large ball starts to form.

Using damp hands to prevent the mixture from sticking too much, pinch off pieces of the mixture about the size of whole walnuts. Roll them into balls between the palms of your hands.

Roll each ball in the desiccated coconut to coat it evenly, then place on a plate or board. Repeat with the rest of the mixture.

Refrigerate for at least 20 minutes. Store in the fridge in an airtight container for up to 3 weeks.

Power green bean balls

You need to plan ahead when making these bean balls, as the broad/fava beans require pre-soaking.

200 g/1 cup dried split broad/fava beans, soaked overnight

5 spring onions/scallions, roughly chopped

3 garlic cloves, peeled

2 tablespoons pumpkin seeds

handful of fresh coriander/cilantro leaves

handful of fresh parsley leaves

1 teaspoon ground cumin

1 teaspoon ground coriander

1 teaspoon baking powder

3 tablespoons chickpea/gram flour

sea salt and freshly ground black pepper

olive oil, for brushing

MAKES 16

Preheat the oven to 180°C (350°F) Gas 4. Line a baking sheet with baking parchment.

Drain the soaked beans and put them in a food processor or blender with the spring onions, garlic, pumpkin seeds and herbs. Process to a coarse paste, occasionally scraping down the mixture from the sides when needed.

Add the spices, baking powder and chickpea flour. Season with salt and pepper to taste and stir to make a coarse paste – it will be slightly wet but will hold together when cooked.

With damp hands, form the mixture into 16 large, walnut-sized balls and put them on the prepared baking sheet. Flatten the tops slightly, brush each one with a little olive oil, then bake for 20–25 minutes, turning once, until firm and golden in places. Serve warm or leave to cool. Store in the fridge in an airtight container for 3–5 days.

Note: these are delicious served with a minty soy yogurt dip.

Super snacks

Miso and ginger give these nutty balls a health boost, as well as a burst of flavour.

50 g/½ cup cashew nuts

50 g/⅓ cup sunflower seeds

40 g/½ cup quinoa flakes or jumbo rolled oats

2 soft dried pitted/stoned dates, chopped

2 teaspoons brown miso paste

1 tablespoon finely grated fresh root ginger

60 g/¼ cup peanut butter

1 tablespoon freshly squeezed lemon juice

cucumber slices, to serve

MAKES 12

Blitz the cashews and sunflower seeds in a food processor or blender until finely chopped. Add the rest of the ingredients and blend to a thick, coarse paste, occasionally scraping down the mixture from the sides when needed.

With damp hands, shape the cashew mixture into 12 walnut-sized balls, then flatten each one into a disc about 2 cm/¾ inch thick. Chill for about 30 minutes to firm up.

Eat straightaway or store the balls (without the cucumber) in the fridge in an airtight container for up to 2 weeks. These super snacks are delicious served with cucumber slices.

Beetroot & ginger balls

These colourful and nutritious balls are full of flavour with an extra kick of fiery ginger.

70 g/2½ oz. peeled raw beetroot/beet, chopped

70 g/½ cup sprouted chickpeas

2 tablespoons pumpkin seeds, roughly chopped, plus extra for topping

4-cm/1½-inch piece of fresh root ginger, peeled and grated

2 soft dried pitted/stoned dates, chopped

50 g/¼ cup cooked quinoa

3 tablespoons ground almonds

2 teaspoons acai powder (optional)

MAKES 10

Put the beetroot, sprouted chickpeas and half the pumpkin seeds in a food processor or blender and process until very finely chopped.

Add the ginger and dates and process again to a thick, smooth-ish paste, occasionally scraping down the mixture from the sides when needed.

Put the cooked quinoa in a mixing bowl and mash roughly with the back of a fork to break down the grains, then add the beetroot mixture, the rest of the pumpkin seeds, the ground almonds and acai powder, if using.

With damp hands, shape the mixture into about 10 walnut-sized balls and top each with a pumpkin seed, if you like. Chill for 30 minutes to firm up. Store in the fridge in an airtight container for up to 5 days.

Himalayan energy bars

The perfect backpack snack! They are nutritionally balanced, high in iron and vitamin C and boast a decent hit of protein.

120 g/1 cup cashew nuts

90 g/⅔ cup walnut halves

140 g/generous 1 cup whole skinless almonds

75 g/½ cup pumpkin seeds, soaked and roughly chopped

25 g/scant ¼ cup pitted/stoned dates, finely chopped

100 g/1⅓ cups desiccated/dried unsweetened shredded coconut

60 g/⅔ cup goji berries

2½ tablespoons date syrup

1 tablespoon chia seeds, soaked in 2 tablespoons water

½ teaspoon sea salt

1 teaspoon vanilla bean paste

30 x 20-cm/12 x 8-inch baking sheet, lined with parchment

MAKES 14

Preheat the oven to 165°C (325°F) Gas 3.

Place half the cashews, walnuts and almonds into a food processor or blender and lightly blitz. Place the remaining nuts onto a chopping board and roughly chop.

Put the blitzed and chopped nuts into a large bowl and add all the remaining ingredients. Using your hands, mix everything really well.

Tip the mixture onto the lined baking sheet. Using the back of a spoon, gently press the mixture into the pan and spread it evenly.

Bake in the preheated oven for 20–25 minutes until just golden brown.

Allow to cool completely before turning out onto a chopping board and peeling off the paper. Using a sharp knife, cut into 14 small bars. The bars will keep for up to 1 week in an airtight container.

Carob & cocoa 'fudge' bars

These magic bars have the creaminess and density of fudge and the nuts provide a wonderful crunch. Carob and cocoa both have distinctive tastes that complement one other.

225 g/1½ cups cashew nuts

100 g/⅔ cup dates, pitted/stoned

80 g/⅔ cup raisins

½ teaspoon ground cinnamon

pinch of sea salt

3 tablespoons raw cocoa powder

3 tablespoons carob powder

60 g/½ cup Brazil nuts, cut into slivers

20-cm/8-inch baking dish, lined with cling film/plastic wrap

MAKES ABOUT 16

Put the cashew nuts, dates and raisins in separate bowls, cover with warm water and allow to soak for 1 hour.

Drain the soaked nuts and fruits and put in a food processor or blender with 4–5 tablespoons water, the cinnamon and salt. Blitz until smooth.

Divide the mixture in half. Add the cocoa to one half and the carob to the other. Mix well.

Spoon the cocoa mixture into the lined baking dish and spread level. Now spoon the carob mixture into the dish on top of the cocoa and spread level. Scatter Brazil nuts evenly over the top, pressing them gently into the fudge. Cover and freeze for at least 2 hours.

You can also refrigerate the fudge but it will remain slightly sticky. It's much easier to slice it when it's frozen, and it tastes a lot better – even better than chocolate ice cream!

Brownie bars

Need a healthy way to satisfy chocolate cravings? Take these five ingredients and blitz yourself a raw, vegan chocolate brownie in no time at all!

300 g/2 cups cashew nuts

120 g/¾ cup walnuts

110 g/1 cup raw cacao powder

100 g/⅔ cup soft dates, pitted/stoned

1 tablespoon coconut oil

agave or pure maple syrup, to taste (optional)

22 x 15-cm/9 x 6-inch deep baking pan or container, lined with baking parchment (optional)

MAKES 6

Put all the ingredients in a food processor or blender and blitz until they are well combined and you have a smooth and rather sticky paste. If it is too dry, add 2 or more tablespoons of agave or maple syrup.

Scrape the mixture into the prepared baking pan and smooth level with your hands. If you don't have the correct size of pan, lay a sheet of cling film/plastic wrap on a board, scrape the mixture onto the sheet and shape it with your hands into a rough rectangle about 2.5 cm/1 inch thick. Wrap in cling film/plastic wrap.

Refrigerate for 1 hour before cutting into about 6 squares to serve.

Spiced fruit bars

These bars are perfect for sustaining energy levels and giving you a boost pre- or post-exercise.

115 g/scant 1 cup roasted hazelnuts, roughly chopped

40 g/½ cup jumbo rolled oats

125 g/1 cup pitted/stoned dried prunes, chopped

70 g/½ cup soft dried apricots, chopped

1 tablespoon chia seeds

2 teaspoons mixed/apple pie spice

1 carrot, grated

2 tablespoons pumpkin seeds, roughly chopped

grated zest and juice of 1 large unwaxed orange

baking pan, lined with cling film/plastic wrap

MAKES 16

Put three-quarters of the hazelnuts in a food processor or blender and blitz until finely chopped. Add the oats and process again until everything is very finely chopped.

Add the prunes and two-thirds of the apricots and process to a smooth-ish paste, occasionally scraping down the mixture from the sides when needed. Stir in the chia seeds, mixed spice, carrot, pumpkin seeds, orange zest and orange juice.

Spoon the fruit mixture into the lined baking pan and spread out with the back of a dampened spoon until it is about 1 cm/½ inch thick.

Cut the remaining apricots into small pieces and scatter over the top. Repeat with the rest of the hazelnuts, pressing the nuts and apricots down slightly to help them stick to the fruit mixture.

Chill for 30 minutes to firm up, then cut into 16 bars, each 2 cm/¾ inch wide. Store in the fridge in an airtight container for up to 2 weeks.

Raspberry, coconut & lemon bars

These energy bars have a slightly softer texture than a flapjack, and the raspberries and lemon add a zingy note.

100 g/¾ cup hazelnuts, roughly chopped

100 g/1 cup rolled/old-fashioned oats

100 g/¾ cup wholemeal/whole-wheat spelt flour

90 g/½ cup coconut sugar

50 g/¾ cup desiccated/dried unsweetened shredded coconut

grated zest and juice of 1 large unwaxed lemon

125 g/½ cup coconut oil

140 g/1 cup frozen raspberries

23-cm/9-inch baking pan, lined with baking parchment

MAKES 16

Preheat the oven to 190°C (375°F) Gas 5.

Put three-quarters of the hazelnuts in a food processor or blender and process until finely chopped. Set aside the remaining chopped nuts.

Put the chopped hazelnuts, oats, flour, coconut sugar, desiccated unsweetened shredded coconut and lemon zest in a mixing bowl.

Gently melt the coconut oil over a low heat, then pour it into the bowl with the lemon juice. Stir until combined, then gently fold in the raspberries.

Transfer the mixture to the prepared pan and scatter over the reserved chopped hazelnuts. Bake for 35–40 minutes, or until firm and light golden. Leave to cool completely in the pan, then lift out, using the parchment to help you. Cut into 16 squares. Store in an airtight container for 3–5 days.

Double ginger nut bites

These bite-sized snacks come with a double dose of ginger, adding a flavour boost plus valuable medicinal properties.

125 g/¾ cup soft dried apricots, chopped

2 tablespoons maple syrup

2 tablespoons coconut oil

90 g/1 cup rolled oats

1 teaspoon ground ginger

2-cm/¾-inch piece of fresh root ginger, peeled and finely grated

20 g/¼ cup pecan nuts, roughly chopped

MAKES 14

Preheat the oven to 180°C (350°F) Gas 4. Line a baking sheet with baking parchment.

Put the apricots in a small pan with 6 tablespoons water and cook, covered, over a low heat until softened, occasionally crushing the apricots with the back of a fork to break them down. This should take 8–10 minutes; the water will be fully absorbed by the fruit.

Transfer the apricots to a food processor or blender with the maple syrup and coconut oil, and blend until puréed.

Mix the oats together with the ground ginger, fresh ginger and pecans in a mixing bowl. Stir in the apricot purée until combined.

With damp hands, shape the apricot mixture into walnut-sized balls and place them on the baking sheet, flattening the top of each one slightly.

Bake for 15–20 minutes until slightly golden around the edges, then transfer to a wire rack to cool. Store in an airtight container for 3–5 days.

Tahini protein bites

A lot of energy-bite snacks use either oats or dried fruit as a base, but what if you want to avoid both? If you're simply looking for a quick way to eat a good protein and fat combo, power up with these bites.

2 scoops vegan protein powder

3 tablespoons coconut flour

¾ tablespoon granulated stevia

3 tablespoons coconut oil

2 tablespoons tahini

½ teaspoon pure vanilla extract

12-hole heart-shaped chocolate mould or silicone ice tray (optional)

MAKES 12

Put the protein powder, coconut flour and stevia in a large mixing bowl and stir to combine.

If your coconut oil is solid, gently melt it in a saucepan set over a medium heat until liquefied.

Pour the melted coconut oil, tahini and vanilla into the dry mixture and stir well.

Scoop the batter into the mould or roll into small balls. Cover and put in the fridge to chill for at least 20 minutes, or until firm.

Turn out the bites from the mould and enjoy.

Sports bites

These light bites packed full of energy-boosting ingredients are the perfect fuel for physical activities where you need a small, compact source of energy that you can easily stop to eat at regular intervals, for instance they would be particularly good to bring on a hike. The natural fruit sugars provide energy and the almonds provide protein, coconut oil and hemp seeds bring the healthy fats, and the coconut oil helps regulate metabolism. All this and they taste amazing too!

50 g/½ cup raw almonds (use raw ones if you can, to make this an all-raw recipe)

60 g/½ cup dried apricots

2 tablespoons shelled hemp seeds

1½ tablespoons coconut oil

vanilla extract, to taste

MAKES 8

Put the almonds in a food processor or blender and pulse until crumbly.

Add the apricots and process until incorporated and the mixture starts to come together into a paste. Add the hemp seeds and coconut oil, plus vanilla extract to taste.

Divide the mixture into 8 and roll each portion into a ball between the palms of your hands.

Freeze the sports bites for at least 15 minutes. Store in the fridge in an airtight container for up to 3 weeks.

Banana oat bites

These require very little effort to make and are perfect for an afternoon boost when energy levels may need perking up.

40 g/½ cup pecan nuts

2 ripe bananas, peeled and chopped

2 teaspoons coconut oil, melted

1 teaspoon pure vanilla extract

90 g/1 cup jumbo rolled oats

2 teaspoons chia seeds

¼ teaspoon sea salt

4 soft dried pitted/stoned dates, chopped

1 teaspoon ground cinnamon

MAKES 10

Preheat the oven to 180°C (350°F) Gas 4. Line a baking sheet with baking parchment.

Toast the pecans in a large, dry frying pan/skillet for 4 minutes, turning once, until they start to colour. Leave to cool, then roughly chop.

Mash the bananas in a mixing bowl to a smooth purée. Stir in all the remaining ingredients and toasted pecans and stir until combined.

Place heaped tablespoonfuls of the mixture onto the prepared baking sheet; the mixture will make around 10. Press down each bite with your fingers into a round about 1 cm/½ inch thick. Bake for 20–25 minutes until golden and crisp.

Leave to cool for 5 minutes before transferring to a wire rack to cool completely. They will keep stored in an airtight container for up to 5 days.

Chapter 3

GRAZING

Salty, crunchy nuts & nibbles

Spicy Cajun mixed nuts

Cashews, pecans and pistachios are listed in the ingredients here, but feel free to choose any nuts you like. Buy them in bulk and you will save money – they won't go to waste as this is a recipe you'll definitely want to make more than once!

140 g/1¼ cups unsalted cashews

140 g/1¼ cups shelled pecans

140 g/1¼ cups shelled pistachios

1 teaspoon cayenne pepper

1 teaspoon pimentón (Spanish smoked paprika)

½ teaspoon dried thyme

1 teaspoon fine sea salt

1 tablespoon soft brown sugar

1 tablespoon olive oil

SERVES 10–12

Preheat the oven to 350°F (180°C) Gas 4. Line a baking sheet with baking parchment.

Put all of the nuts in a large bowl. Add the cayenne pepper, paprika, thyme, salt and sugar and mix to combine. Stir in the olive oil. Tip the nuts out onto the lined baking sheet, spreading them out into a single layer.

Bake in the preheated oven for 10 minutes, stirring halfway through the cooking time. Leave to cool completely before serving.

The nuts are great served with drinks or as a snack. They will keep well for 7–10 days if stored in an airtight container.

Salty trail mix

This trail mix is a very satisfying blend of nuts, seeds and succulent fruits – great for snacking.

100 g/⅔ cup almonds

100 g/⅔ cup pecans

100 g/⅔ cup sunflower seeds

50 g/⅓ cup pumpkin seeds

3 tablespoons goji berries

3 tablespoons raisins

2–3 tablespoons pure maple syrup

1 teaspoon sea salt, or to taste

non-stick dehydrator sheet

dehydrator

SERVES 2–4

Soak the almonds and pecans in separate bowls of cold water for 4 hours; and the sunflower seeds and pumpkin seeds in separate bowls of cold water for 30 minutes.

Drain the nuts and seeds and toss with the remaining ingredients in a bowl.

Spread the mix out on the dehydrator sheet. Dehydrate at 46°C/115°F for 20–24 hours, flipping the mix over halfway through. It is ready to enjoy when the nuts and seeds are crunchy. Store in an airtight container until needed.

Variation: You can also make some spicy almonds in the dehydrator. Soak 150 g/1¼ cups almonds in a bowl of cold water for 6 hours. Thoroughly drain, then toss with 1 tablespoon maple syrup, 2 teaspoons chilli/chili powder, 1½ teaspoons finely grated onion, ¾ teaspoon ground cumin and ½ teaspoon salt in a bowl to coat evenly. Dehydrate as above.

Thai green curry popcorn

Full of the enticing flavours of Thai cuisine, this popcorn is one satisfying snack.

100 g/6 tablespoons extra virgin coconut oil, plus 1–2 tablespoons for cooking the popcorn

90 g/⅓ cup popcorn kernels

1 tablespoon vegan Thai green curry paste

1 teaspoon lemongrass purée (see Note below)

grated zest of 1 lime

2 teaspoons sugar

1 generous tablespoon freshly chopped coriander/cilantro

sea salt and freshly ground black pepper

SERVES 6

Heat 1–2 tablespoons of the coconut oil in a large lidded saucepan with a few popcorn kernels in the pan with the lid on. When you hear the kernels pop, carefully tip in the rest of the kernels and replace the lid. Shake the pan over the heat until the popping stops. Take care when lifting the lid as any unpopped kernels may pop from the heat of the pan. Tip the popcorn into a bowl, removing any unpopped kernels as you go.

Melt the remaining extra virgin coconut oil in a small saucepan set over a low heat. Add the curry paste, lemongrass purée and lime zest and cook for a few minutes, stirring all the time.

Pour the Thai-flavoured coconut oil over the warm popcorn, sprinkle with the sugar, coriander, salt and pepper, and stir well so that the popcorn is evenly coated. Can be eaten warm or cold.

Note: Lemongrass purée is available in most supermarkets, but if you are unable to find it you can substitute a 2-cm/1-inch piece of lemongrass, chopped and pounded in a mortar and pestle with 1 tablespoon vegetable oil.

Taralli

These tasty bites are tradtionally served as an aperitif, but they make excellent an snack at any time of day.

150 g/1 cup plus 2 tablespoons Italian '00' flour, plus extra for sprinkling and kneading

40 g/⅓ cup semolina (fine)

1 teaspoon freshly ground black pepper or 2 teaspoons lightly crushed fennel seeds (optional)

2 teaspoons sea salt

70 ml/⅓ cup dry white wine

70 ml/⅓ cup extra virgin olive oil

MAKES 30

Mix together the flour, semolina, pepper or fennel seeds, half the salt, wine and oil. Knead on a floured surface for about 2 minutes until smooth and elastic. Place the dough in a lightly oiled bowl, cover and leave to relax for about 45–60 minutes.

Halve the dough and cut each half into 10 pieces. Keep the remaining dough covered with a damp kitchen cloth while you work. Roll one piece of dough into a 50-cm/10-inch long rope. Cut the rope into 5 pieces, then roll each piece into 10-cm/4-inch ropes. Connect the ends to form an overlapping ring. Continue with the remaining dough, keeping the taralli covered.

Preheat the oven to 180°C (350°F) Gas 5. Bring 900 ml/scant 4 cups water to the boil and add the remaining salt.

Boil the rings in batches for about 3 minutes until they float. Transfer with a slotted spoon to oiled baking sheets and bake in the oven for 30 minutes until golden. Cool on wire racks, then enjoy.

Spicy tomato kale chips

These kale chips are moreish but beautifully light too, so eating too many in one go is not a problem!

1 head of curly kale or 1 packet of pre-chopped curly kale (about 50 g/1¾ oz.), torn into small pieces and washed and thoroughly dried

1 large tomato, quartered

3 sun-dried tomatoes (dry not marinated ones, with no added sugar)

½ teaspoon paprika

¼ teaspoon ground cumin

pinch of sea salt

⅛–¼ teaspoon cayenne pepper

freshly ground black pepper

SERVES 6

Preheat the oven to 200°C (400°F) Gas 6. Line a baking sheet with foil.

Place the dry kale pieces in a large bowl.

Put the tomato and sun-dried tomatoes in a food processor. Pulse until smooth, scraping down the sides of the bowl as you go.

Add the paprika, cumin and salt, then as much cayenne and black pepper as you like, depending on how spicy you want your chips to turn out. Process the mixture again, then pour it into the bowl of kale. Using your hands, toss the kale so that it is evenly coated in the tomato mixture.

Spread the kale pieces onto the prepared baking sheet and bake in the preheated oven with the door slightly ajar for about 14–16 minutes. You will know the kale is ready when it is totally crispy and thin. If you can resist eating it all immediately, store it in an airtight container for about 4–5 days at room temperature.

Oven-baked rosemary crisps/chips

DIY oven crisps/chips are way prettier than the ones that come in a package. Using a mandoline for slicing your veg is highly recommended so they crisp up well when cooked.

2 small-medium beetroot/beets, very thinly sliced

1 sweet potato, white potato or purple potato, very thinly sliced

olive oil, for brushing

1 tablespoon fresh rosemary leaves, finely chopped

sea salt

hummus, to serve

SERVES 3–4

Preheat the oven to 190°C (375°F) Gas 5. Brush 2 baking sheets with oil

Arrange the individual beetroot and potato slices on the prepared baking sheets, giving each slice plenty of space.

Lightly brush the vegetables with olive oil, sprinkle with rosemary and season with salt to taste.

Bake in the oven for 10–13 minutes, watching them carefully to make sure they don't burn.

Remove from the oven and let the crisps cool on the sheets before transferring to a serving plate or bowl. Repeat with any remaining vegetables as necessary. Serve with a big bowl of hummus for dipping, if you like.

Cajun tortilla chips

Super-easy corn chips without the usual additives and flavourings, which are often found in shop-bought versions. They are flavoured with a homemade Cajun spice mix, but you could use ready-made if short on time.

4 corn tortillas

½ teaspoon spirulina powder (optional)

1 teaspoon sesame seeds

sea salt

extra-virgin olive oil, for brushing

CAJUN SPICE MIX

1 teaspoon dried oregano

1 tablespoon paprika

2 teaspoons ground turmeric

½ teaspoon chilli/chili powder

2 teaspoons ground cumin

1 teaspoon garlic granules/ powder

SERVES 4

Preheat the oven to 180°C (350°F) Gas 4.

Mix together all the ingredients for the Cajun spice mix.

Place the tortillas directly on the shelves in the oven, spacing them apart so they don't touch each other. Bake for about 8 minutes, turning once, until crisp and golden in places. Remove from the oven and place on a wire rack.

Brush one side of each tortilla with oil and sprinkle over ¼ teaspoon of the Cajun spice mix, as well as the spirulina, if using, and some sesame seeds. Cut into wedges, then leave to cool and crisp up. They will keep in an airtight container for up to 2 days.

Note: You'll have leftovers of the Cajun spice mix, but it keeps well in a lidded jar for a couple of months or so.

Nori miso crisps

Very easy and very moreish... these crispy strips of nori are flavoured with brown miso and sprinkled with sesame seeds. You can also flavour them with wasabi paste.

2 teaspoons brown miso paste, or type of your choice

3 toasted nori sheets

½ teaspoon super-greens powder

½ teaspoon sesame seeds

MAKES 24

Preheat the oven to 160°C (325°F) Gas 3. Line a baking sheet with baking parchment.

Mix the miso paste with 2 teaspoons water and brush it over one half of each sheet of nori. Sprinkle the super-greens powder and the sesame seeds over the miso-coated nori.

Fold the nori sheet in half to encase the filling and press down lightly so the two halves stick together. Cut each sheet of nori into 8 strips, each 2 cm/¾ inch wide, and place on the prepared baking sheet. Cook in the oven for 5–7 minutes until crisp.

Leave to cool on the baking sheet, then eat straightaway or store in an airtight container for up to 1 day. They will keep for longer but tend to lose their crispness over time.

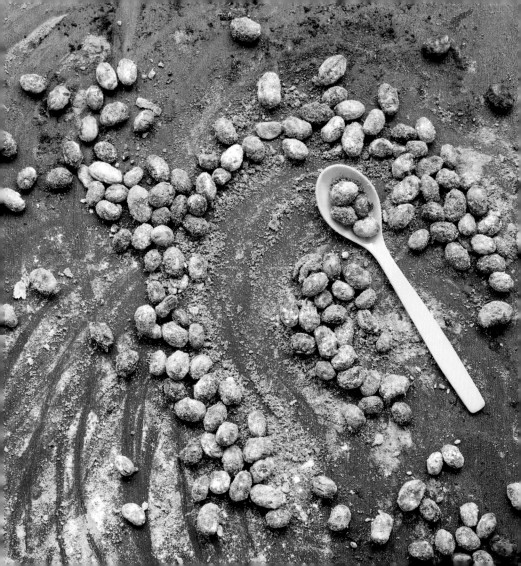

Wasabi-roasted edamame

Edamame are a complete protein, meaning they contain all nine essential amino acids and are brimming with minerals.

150 g/1 cup frozen edamame beans, defrosted

2 teaspoons cold-pressed rapeseed oil

1 teaspoon wasabi powder, or to taste

sea salt

MAKES 1 CUP

Preheat the oven to 180°C (350°F) Gas 4. Line a baking sheet with baking parchment.

Pat dry the edamame with paper towels and place on the prepared baking sheet. Pour the oil over the beans, toss with your hands until they are coated, then spread out on the baking sheet. Toast in the oven for 15 minutes, then remove and sprinkle the wasabi powder over them and season with salt. Turn the edamame until coated in the wasabi and return to the oven for another 15–20 minutes until crisp and golden.

Sprinkle over more wasabi or salt, to taste, if needed. Leave on the baking sheet to cool and crisp up further. Store in an airtight container for up to 3 days.

Variation: Chickpeas also work well and crisp up in the oven to make a tasty snack. Simply rinse, drain and pat dry a 400-g/14-oz. can of chickpeas. Coat in 1 tablespoon olive oil and 2 teaspoons spice mix of your choice, and roast in the same way as the edamame above.

Chickpea fritters

Known in Sicily as *panelle*, these fritters are both soft on the inside and crunchy on the outside; the perfect snack.

250 g/2 cups chickpea/gram flour, sifted

1 tablespoon freshly chopped flat-leaf parsley

3 tablespoons olive oil

coarse sea salt and freshly ground black pepper

SERVES 4–6

Whisk the chickpea flour into 1 litre/4 cups water until lump-free, then season with 1 teaspoon salt.

Heat the batter gently in a saucepan, stirring constantly, until it boils and thickens. Simmer for about 15 minutes, whisking constantly. Stir in the parsley and cook for another 5 minutes.

Pour onto a baking sheet lined with baking parchment and level the surface. The mixture should be no more than 1 cm/⅜ inch thick. Leave to cool for several hours to allow the mixture to solidify. Cut the set batter into triangles or squares.

Preheat the oven to 200°C (400°F) Gas 6.

When the oven is hot, put the olive oil on a clean baking sheet and heat in the oven for a few minutes, then transfer the fritters to the hot oil, flipping over once to coat both sides with oil. Bake in the oven for 20 minutes, until the fritters are crisp on the surface and starting to brown, then turn over and cook for another 10 minutes. Sprinkle with salt and pepper and serve immediately.

'Cheesy' pumpkin crackers

Nutritional yeast flakes don't sound particularly appetizing, but they are nutritionally abundant and, despite being dairy-free, have a distinctly cheesy flavour that makes a useful addition to a vegan diet.

90 g/²⁄₃ cup pumpkin seeds

2 large garlic cloves, skins peeled

10 g/¼ oz. poppy seeds or flaxseeds/linseeds

½ teaspoon sea salt

15 g/½ oz. nutritional yeast flakes

1½ teaspoons caraway seeds

1 tablespoon extra-virgin olive oil

freshly ground black pepper

MAKES 16

Preheat the oven to 190°C (375°F) Gas 5. Line a baking sheet with baking parchment.

Put the pumpkin seeds and garlic in a food processor and process to a coarse paste. Add the rest of the ingredients with 3½ tablespoons water, season with pepper and blend until the mixture starts to come together in a ball of dough.

Form the dough into a flattened rectangle and place between2 sheets of baking parchment. Using a rolling pin, roll the dough into a thin rectangle, about 3 mm/⅛ inch thick, and mark the dough into 16 5-cm/2-inch squares with the pointed-end of a knife. Place on the lined baking sheet and bake for about 20–25 minutes until light golden and firm.

Using the marked lines, cut into 16 squares and remove from the baking sheet, using the baking parchment to help you. Leave to cool on a wire rack, then separate into individual crackers. Store in an airtight container for 3–5 days.

Chapter 4

BAR BITES

Tasty snacks to enjoy with a drink

Gourd & cashew koftas

These koftas make a great sharing platter for a buffet or family feast and the pomegranate raita is an eye-catching addition.

2 bottle/doodhi gourds, peeled and grated

375 g/3 cups chickpea/gram flour

2 red chillies/chiles, chopped

120 g/1 cup cashew nuts, toasted

1 teaspoon each of ginger paste and garlic paste

handful of coriander/cilantro

1 teaspoon chaat masala

1 teaspoon sea salt, or to taste

vegetable oil, for shallow-frying

FOR THE RAITA

500 g/2 cups soya/soy yogurt

bunch of fresh mint leaves, chopped

½ teaspoon mint sauce

pomegranate seeds, to serve

SERVES 4–6

To make the raita, put the yogurt in a small bowl and add the mint and mint sauce. Stir to combine. Stir in the pomegranate seeds. Set aside.

For the koftas, put the grated gourds into a colander and drain the excess liquid, squeezing to remove as much water as possible. Put the flour into a bowl and add the chillies, cashews, ginger and garlic pastes, coriander, chaat masala and salt. Add 240–360 ml/1–1½ cups water to form a thick paste. Add more salt if needed.

Half-fill a frying pan/skillet with vegetable oil and place over a medium heat. Test the oil temperature by dropping a little batter into the oil, when it rises to the top and sizzles without burning, the oil is ready for frying.

Use wet hands to form the kofta mixture into 16–18 loose balls, each about the size of a golf ball. Gently drop the koftas into the hot oil (do not overcrowd the pan) and fry in batches for about 6–8 minutes until golden brown and cooked through. Drain on paper towels and serve with the raita.

Heart of palm 'calamari'

You can flavour the batter with whatever spicing you like or keep it simple served with nothing more than lemon wedges.

200 g/7 oz. can heart of palm 'rings', rinsed and drained

1 tablespoon rice flour

1 tablespoon potato flour

1 tablespoon plain/all-purpose flour

½ teaspoon sea salt

2 tablespoons Korean red pepper flakes or powder

150 ml/⅔ cup sparkling water, plus extra if needed

300–400 ml/1¼–scant 1¾ cups vegetable oil, for deep-frying

TO SERVE

lemon wedges

vegan aioli

SERVES 3–4

Slice the heart of palm rings into 2.5-cm/1-inch rounds. Carefully push out the centre of each ring with your fingertip (this flaky part of the palm is perfect for making a vegan ravioli filling if liked). Repeat with the other rounds.

Mix the rice, potato and plain flour together in a small bowl and add the salt and Korean red pepper flakes or powder. Add 150 ml/⅔ cup of the sparkling water and mix well to form a runny batter that should coat the back of a spoon. Add more sparkling water, if needed.

Preheat the oven to 120°C (250°F) Gas ½.

Heat the oil for deep-frying in a small frying pan/skillet until about 190°C/375°F. Check the oil temperature with a small drop of batter; it should sizzle but not burn. Dip the heart of palm rings into the batter to coat, then carefully drop into the hot oil, frying in batches for 2–3 minutes until golden and crispy. Drain on paper towels.

Put the cooked rings in the low oven to keep warm while frying the remaining batches. Serve immediately with lemon wedges and aioli.

Jalapeño onion rings

This grown up, healthier version of the traditional fried bar snack is a real crowd pleaser.

3 tablespoons ground flaxseeds/linseeds

170 g/1 cup cornmeal/polenta

150 g/1 cup gluten-free crackers, processed into crumbs

1 large fresh jalapeño pepper, thinly sliced and deseeded if you don't like things too spicy

½ teaspoon sea salt

freshly ground black pepper

2 large onions, cut into 2-cm/1-inch thick slices

MAKES ABOUT 36

Preheat the oven to 220°C (425°F) Gas 7. Line 2 baking sheet with foil.

Mix the flaxseeds with 175 ml/⅔ cup water and set aside.

In a separate bowl, mix the cornmeal, cracker crumbs, jalapeño, salt and pepper to taste in a wide bowl.

Separate the onion slices into rings. Dip them into the flaxseed mixture, then into the crumb mixture. For each onion ring, do this twice so that they are double-coated.

Arrange the rings on the prepared baking sheets and bake in the preheated oven for 8–12 minutes until they are slightly browned on the outside and cooked all the way through.

Marinated olives & padrón peppers

These olives are made in advance but the padrón peppers need to be cooked and then served straight away.

QUICK MARINATED OLIVES

200 ml/¾ cup good-quality olive oil

3 garlic cloves, bruised and skin on

large sprig of fresh rosemary

1 hot red chilli/chile, thinly sliced

grated zest of 1 lemon

400-g/14-oz. black pitted/stoned olives

PADRÓN PEPPERS

20 pimientos de Padrón (small green fresh Spanish peppers), washed and dried

1 tablespoon good olive oil

sea salt

SERVES 4–6

To make the olives, put the oil, garlic and rosemary in a saucepan and heat very gently, until the first few bubbles begin to rise up to the surface. Remove the pan from the heat, add the chilli and lemon zest and set aside to cool.

Meanwhile, drain, rinse and pat the olives dry on paper towels. Place them in a large jar or bowl. Once the infused olive oil has cooled, pour it over the drained olives. Leave at room temperature for at least 2 hours before serving, occasionally stirring or shaking (if they are in a jar!) to allow the flavours to infuse the olives.

To make the Padrón peppers, heat the oil in a frying pan/skillet over a medium heat and fry the peppers in small batches, turning frequently, until they begin to change colour and the skin starts to puff up. Remove from the pan and drain on paper towels. Season with salt flakes and serve.

Cauli 'cheese' bites

This simple snack will definitely hit the spot when you are craving something 'cheesy'.

5 teaspoons olive oil

1 teaspoon ground turmeric

250 g/3½ cups cauliflower florets

sea salt and freshly ground black pepper

VEGAN 'PARMESAN'
50 g/½ cup pecan nuts

3 tablespoons nutritional yeast flakes

MAKES 250 G/3½ CUPS

Preheat the oven to 190°C (375°F) Gas 5. Line a baking sheet with baking parchment.

Mix together the olive oil and turmeric and season with salt and pepper.

Put the cauliflower in a bowl, pour over the turmeric mixture and turn until the florets are coated all over. Tip them onto the prepared baking sheet, spread out evenly and roast for 25–30 minutes, turning once, until tender and starting to colour.

While the cauli is roasting, make the vegan 'Parmesan'. Blitz the pecans and nutritional yeast flakes in a coffee or spice grinder to a coarse powder.

Spoon 2 tablespoons of the vegan 'Parmesan' over the roasted cauli and turn until evenly coated. (Any leftover 'Parmesan' will keep in the fridge in an airtight container for up to 2 weeks.) The bites are best eaten warm but can be cooled and kept, covered, in the fridge for up to 2 days.

Japanese rice balls

Brown rice has a lovely nutty flavour and using short-grain rather than long-grain rice will help these balls stick together.

175 g/6 oz. short-grain brown rice, rinsed well

2 teaspoons black sesame seeds

2 teaspoons hulled hemp seeds

¼ teaspoon togarashi spice mix, plus extra for sprinkling (optional)

½ sheet toasted nori, cut into 10 strips, each about 4 x 1 cm/ 1½ x ½ inch in size

sea salt

FILLINGS (OPTIONAL)
Japanese pickles, cut into small pieces

kimchi, finely chopped

smoked tofu, cut into small cubes

MAKES 10

Put the rice in a pan. Pour over enough water to cover the rice by about 1 cm/½ inch. Bring to the boil. Cover the pan with a lid, turn the heat to its lowest setting and cook for 20–25 minutes until the rice is tender and the water has been absorbed. Turn off the heat and leave to stand for 15 minutes.

Mix together the black sesame seeds, hemp seeds and togarashi, then stir the mixture into the rice.

To make filled onigiri, put the rice in the centre of the cling film/plastic wrap and press it into a disc with wet fingers. Place a piece of pickle, kimchi or smoked tofu in the centre and shape the rice around, using the cling film to help, to encase the filling. Next, shape the rice into a triangle or ball shape as preferred.

Remove the cling film and stick a strip of nori around the base, then finish with a sprinkling of togarashi on top, if liked. Eat straightaway or store, covered, in the fridge for up to 2 days.

Courgette un-fries

Inspired by the moreish deep-fried courgette/zucchini side dish served in some restaurants, this brilliant snack version is baked instead of fried.

80 ml/⅓ cup almond milk

35 g/¼ cup quinoa flour

35 g/¼ cup ground flaxseeds/linseeds

1 teaspoon garlic powder

½ teaspoon onion powder

½ teaspoon freshly ground black pepper

½ teaspoon sea salt

2 large courgettes/zucchini, cut into 5-mm/¼-inch slices

SERVES 3–4

Preheat the oven to 220°C (425°F) Gas 7. Line a baking sheet with baking parchment.

Put the almond milk in a bowl and set aside.

Put all the remaining ingredients (except the courgettes) in a separate, wide bowl and mix well.

Dip each slice of courgette into the almond milk, one at a time, then dip into the dry mixture. Once fully coated, place on the prepared baking sheet.

Bake the fries in the oven for 15 minutes. Remove from the oven, flip the slices over and bake for another 15 minutes. Keep a close eye on them, as they burn easily.

They can be served warm from the oven or at room temperature. Store in an airtight container for up to 3 days.

Creole cauliflower

Creole rub is a mix of southern American flavours normally used to flavour meat; it gives a fantastic zing to these bites.

1 large head of cauliflower, cut into florets about 1 cm/ ½ inch thick

2 tablespoons black treacle/ molasses or maple syrup

4–5 tablespoons tomato passata/strained tomatoes (or 1 tablespoon tomato paste mixed with 4 tablespoons water if you don't have passata on hand)

1 teaspoon cayenne pepper

2 teaspoons paprika

1 teaspoon ground cumin

½ teaspoon dried thyme

½ teaspoon garlic powder

1 teaspoon sea salt

freshly ground black pepper

SERVES 6

Preheat the oven to 115°C (225°F) Gas ¼, with the fan on, if possible. Line a baking sheet with baking parchment.

Wash the cauliflower florets thoroughly, then place in a large bowl. Put all the remaining ingredients in a separate, wide bowl and mix well.

Pour the mixture over the cauliflower in the bowl and toss until well coated.

Scatter the cauliflower on the prepared baking sheet and bake in the preheated oven for about 6 hours, until thoroughly dried and crisp.

Aubergine & sumac fries

Zingy, zesty and fresh, these 'fries' are a real treat enhanced by the velvety smooth texture of aubergine/eggplant.

500 g/1 lb. 2 oz. aubergine/eggplant, ends trimmed and cut into 2-cm/¾-inch wide strips

125 g/1 cup rice flour

1 tablespoon sumac, plus extra to serve

1 teaspoon fine salt

vegetable oil, for frying

1 tablespoon toasted sesame seeds

2–3 sprigs fresh mint, leaves stripped and very finely chopped

lemon wedges and tahini mixed with soy yogurt, to serve (optional)

SERVES 2–4 AS A SIDE

A few hours before serving (ideally 2–12 hours), put the aubergine in a large bowl and add cold water and some ice to cover. Set a plate on top to weigh the aubergine down; it must stay submerged.

When ready to cook, combine the rice flour, sumac and salt in a bowl and mix well.

Fill a large saucepan one-third full with the oil or, if using a deep-fat fryer, follow the manufacturer's instructions. Heat the oil to 190°C (375°F) or until a cube of bread browns in about 30 seconds.

Working in batches, transfer the damp aubergine to the rice flour mixture and coat lightly. Place in a frying basket and lower into the hot oil carefully. Fry for about 3–4 minutes until golden. Remove and drain on paper towels. Repeat until all of the aubergine has been fried.

Mound on a platter and scatter over the sesame seeds, some sumac and the mint leaves. Serve with lemon wedges and tahini yogurt if liked.

Dukkah bean balls

These kidney bean balls can be eaten as a snack on their own or dunked into hummus, guacamole or a mint yogurt dip. Alternatively, stuff them into a wrap, taco shell or pitta bread with lots of salad for a full meal.

1 small onion, chopped

2 garlic cloves, peeled

400-g/14-oz. can red kidney beans, drained and rinsed

40 g/1½ oz. carrot, finely grated

2 teaspoons chickpea/gram flour

2 tablespoons dukkah

sea salt and freshly ground black pepper

olive oil, for brushing

MAKES 10

Put the onion and garlic in a food processor and blitz to a coarse paste. Add the kidney beans and process again to make a coarse purée (you want to retain some chunks of kidney bean), occasionally scraping the mixture down the sides when needed. Stir in the carrot, chickpea flour and dukkah, then season with salt and pepper.

With damp hands, form the mixture into about 10 walnut-sized balls, place on a baking sheet lined with baking parchment and chill for about 30 minutes to firm up.

Preheat the oven to 190°C (375°F) Gas 5.

Generously brush the balls with olive oil and bake in the oven for 25 minutes, turning occasionally, or until golden brown all over. Eat warm or cold. The balls will keep stored in the fridge in an airtight container for up to 3 days.

Sweet potato & quinoa bites

The addition of ginger gives a warming, zingy lift to these moreish bite-sized balls making them hard to resist.

400 g/14 oz. sweet potato, peeled and cut into large chunks

70 g/2½ oz. cooked quinoa

2.5-cm/1-inch piece of fresh root ginger, grated (no need to peel)

2 garlic cloves, finely chopped

handful of freshly chopped coriander/cilantro leaves

2 teaspoons ras el hanout

3 tablespoons almond flour

sea salt and freshly ground black pepper

cold-pressed rapeseed oil, for brushing

2 baking sheets, lined with baking parchment and lightly greased with cold-pressed rapeseed oil

MAKES 20

Steam the sweet potato for 10–15 minutes until tender. Leave to cool slightly, then coarsely grate the sweet potato into a mixing bowl. Add the cooked quinoa to the bowl and roughly mash with the back of a fork to break the grains down slightly. Stir in the ginger, garlic, coriander, ras el hanout and almond flour. Season the mixture with salt and pepper, and stir in a little water if needed to bring everything together.

Rather than rolling the mixture into balls in your hands, use a tablespoon as a mould – take heaped tablespoons of the sweet potato mixture and 'plop' them out in mounds onto the prepared baking sheets. Chill them for 30 minutes to firm up.

Preheat the oven to 190°C (375°F) Gas 5.

Brush the tops of the bites with cold-pressed rapeseed oil and bake for 25–30 minutes until crisp on the outside and light golden. Eat warm or cold. Store in the fridge in an airtight container for 3–5 days.

Chapter 5

SWEET TREATS

A little bit of what you fancy

Coffee cookies

The irresistible cookies are perfect for coffee lovers

30 g/⅓ cup raw cocoa beans

100 g/½ cup coconut oil, softened

100 g/½ cup Demerara sugar

60 ml/¼ cup plain soy milk

2 teaspoons coffee extract

¼ teaspoon apple cider vinegar

200 g/1½ cups spelt flour

½ teaspoon baking powder

1 tablespoon ground flaxseeds

¼ teaspoon bourbon vanilla powder

2 tablespoons ground almonds

¼ teaspoon sea salt

¼ teaspoon ground cinnamon

FOR TOPPING (OPTIONAL)
tahini, for drizzling

chopped nuts

MAKES 25

Preheat the oven to 180°C (350°F) Gas 4. Line 2 baking sheets with baking parchment.

Grind the cocoa beans in a coffee or spice grinder to a fine powder.

Whisk together the coconut oil, sugar, milk, coffee extract and vinegar. In a separate bowl, sift together the flour and baking powder, then stir in the flaxseeds, vanilla powder, ground almonds, salt, cinnamon and ground cocoa beans or nibs. Tip into the bowl of wet ingredients and mix into a smooth dough.

Divide the dough into 25 and roll into balls. Arrange on the baking sheets about 2 cm/¾ inch apart and gently flatten each ball. Bake in the oven for 9–10 minutes – they should still be a little soft. Allow to cool on the baking sheets.

Drizzle a little tahini over the cooled cookies (if using) and sprinkle with nuts. Store in an airtight container at room temperature, or, in the summer months, in the fridge. They will keep for up to 2 weeks.

Coconut cookies

These luxurious cookies will not last long in any household and the oval shape makes these perfect for dunking!

130 g/1 cup unbleached spelt or plain/all-purpose flour

¼ teaspoon bicarbonate of/baking soda

¼ teaspoon sea salt

¼ teaspoon bourbon vanilla powder

160 g/2 cups desiccated coconut

75 g/⅓ cup coconut or soy milk

135 g/⅔ cup Demerara sugar

65 g/⅓ cup coconut oil

1 tablespoon ground flaxseeds (optional)

50 g/⅓ cup vegan dark/bittersweet chocolate, melted

MAKES ABOUT 20

Preheat the oven to 180°C (350°F) Gas 4. Line a baking sheet with baking parchment. Sift the flour, bicarbonate of soda, salt and vanilla powder into a bowl, then stir in the coconut.

Put the milk, sugar, oil and flaxseeds (if using) in a separate bowl and whisk vigorously until well combined. Pour into the bowl of dry ingredients and mix until you get dough that is firm but a little sticky and not too dry or crumbly.

Using wet hands, pull off a tablespoon of the dough and roll into a sausage and then flatten to get a flat, oval cookie. Continue with the rest of the dough, arranging each cookie 2 cm/¾ inch apart on the baking sheet. Bake for 8–10 minutes, no longer! Take them out as soon as the bottoms turn slightly golden. Don't worry if they seem soft – they will harden as they cool. Transfer to a wire rack and allow to cool completely.

Drizzle the melted chocolate over the cooled cookies and allow to set. Store in an airtight container for up to 2 weeks.

Chocolate banana bread

The perfect vegan banana bread for a snack at any time of day.

130 g/1 cup wholemeal/whole-wheat flour

100 g/1 cup almond flour

50 g/½ cup oat flour

3 teaspoons baking powder

1 teaspoon ground cinnamon

½ teaspoon ground nutmeg

½ teaspoon sea salt

3 large bananas (overripe is best)

90 ml/⅓ cup melted coconut oil

60 ml/¼ cup almond milk

1 teaspoon vanilla extract

60 ml/¼ cup pure maple syrup

80 g/½ cup vegan dark/bittersweet chocolate chips

30 g/¼ cup pecans or walnuts

12 x 23-cm/9 x 5-inch loaf pan, greased with coconut oil

MAKES 1 LOAF

Preheat the oven to 180°C (350°F) Gas 4.

Mix together the dry ingredients (flours, baking powder, spices and salt) in a medium bowl.

Mash the bananas in another bowl, then add the melted coconut oil, almond milk, vanilla and maple syrup and mix everything together using a rubber spatula.

Gradually mix the dry ingredients into the banana mixture until everything is well combined. Fold in the chocolate chips.

Pour the batter into the prepared loaf pan and sprinkle the top with the pecans or walnuts. Bake the loaf in the preheated oven for 45–50 minutes, rotating halfway through the cooking time.

Remove from the oven and leave to cool to room temperature in the pan before turning out. Serve toasted with nut butter if liked.

Almond butter cups

Peanut butter and chocolate is a great combo, but actually almond butter works better in this recipe.

215 ml/1 cup coconut oil

60 g/¾ cup unsweetened cocoa powder

4 tablespoons agave syrup

1 tablespoon stevia (or 2 more tablespoons agave syrup)

dash of vanilla extract

4–5 tablespoons almond butter

1 teaspoon nutritional yeast

pinch of sea salt (if using unsalted almond butter)

12-hole muffin pan, or 24-hole mini muffin pan, lined with paper cases

MAKES 12 LARGE CUPS, OR 24 MINI CUPS

Put the coconut oil in a saucepan over a low heat and allow to melt. Stir in the cocoa powder, agave syrup, stevia, if using, and vanilla extract until you have smooth liquid chocolate. Divide one-third of the mixture between the muffin cases and put the whole muffin pan in the freezer for about 5 minutes until the mixture has solidified.

Meanwhile, mix the almond butter, nutritional yeast and salt, if needed, in a bowl.

Remove the muffin pan from the freezer and place a generous teaspoon of the almond-yeast mixture in the centre of each base of frozen chocolate, then flatten it slightly with your fingers. Pour the remaining melted chocolate over the almond-yeast mixture. Put the whole muffin pan in the freezer again for 10 minutes, or until the mixture has solidified.

Remove from the freezer just before serving to get them at their most firm and crisp. If you store them in the freezer or fridge, they will keep for 3–4 weeks (unless you devour them before!).

Chocolate chip cooies

These chewy cookies have just the right amount of sweetness and use protein-rich flour for added sustenance.

2 tablespoons ground chia seeds

120 ml/½ cup gently melted coconut oil

100 g/½ cup coconut sugar or soft light brown sugar

1 teaspoon vanilla extract

185 g/1½ cups chickpea/gram flour

1 teaspoon baking powder

¼ teaspoon sea salt

50 g/⅓ cup vegan dark/bittersweet chocolate chips

flaky sea salt, for sprinkling

MAKES ABOUT 12

Combine the chia seeds with 90 ml/⅓ cup water in a bowl and whisk to a gel-like consistency. Add the coconut oil, sugar and vanilla. Whisk with a hand-held electric whisk until combined.

In a separate medium bowl, combine the chickpea flour, baking powder and salt. Add these dry ingredients to the wet ingredients and mix to combine everything using a rubber spatula. (Your cookie batter will be quite wet, but don't worry.) Stir in the chocolate until evenly dispersed. Chill to firm up for 30–60 minutes.

Preheat the oven to 180°C (350°F) Gas 4. Line a baking sheet with baking parchment.

Scoop the mixture into ping pong-sized balls and space evenly apart on the prepared baking sheet. Press each cookie gently to flatten them slightly. Sprinkle each cookie with a small pinch of sea salt. Bake for 11–12 minutes. Leave to cool on the baking sheet for 5–10 minutes, then transfer to a wire rack to cool fully. Store in an airtight container at room temperature for up to 5 days.

Cocoa-almond freezer fudge pops

This frozen, chocolatey concoction is a great way to 'upgrade' your vegan chocolate fix, and especially good after dinner on a warm summer's evening straight from the freezer.

70 ml/¼ cup almond butter (drain off the oil before measuring)

2 teaspoons ground flaxseeds/linseeds

1 large teaspoon coconut oil

1 large teaspoon xylitol

1½ tablespoons raw unsweetened cocoa powder, plus extra for dusting

½ teaspoon vanilla extract

1 teaspoon espresso powder (optional)

MAKES 8

Put all the ingredients in a food processor or blender and blitz until smooth.

Divide the mixture into 8 and roll each portion into a ball between the palms of your hands. Dust in cocoa powder.

Freeze the fudge pops for at least 30 minutes and consume straight from the freezer. Store in the freezer for up to 4 weeks.

Coconut & cherry drops

Similar to coconut macaroons, these come with a health boost thanks to the addition of ground flaxseeds/linseeds and sesame seeds.

85 g/3 oz. desiccated/dried unsweetened shredded coconut

25 g/1 oz. coconut sugar

1 tablespoon ground flaxseeds/linseeds

25 g/1 oz. ground almonds

2 tablespoons aquafaba (liquid from a can of chickpeas)

1 teaspoon toasted sesame seeds

14 dried sour cherries

MAKES 14

Preheat the oven to 180°C (350°F) Gas 4. Line a baking sheet with baking parchment.

Mix together the coconut, coconut sugar, ground flaxseeds and ground almonds in a bowl.

Whisk the aquafaba in a grease-free mixing bowl until it forms soft peaks. Gently fold the coconut mixture into the aquafaba one-third at a time, taking care not to lose too much air, until incorporated.

Using a tablespoon, place rounded scoops of the mixture onto the prepared baking sheet. Sprinkle with a few sesame seeds and place a cherry on top of each one.

Bake for about 10–12 minutes until golden and firm. Leave to cool on the baking sheet for 5 minutes before transferring to a wire rack to cool completely. The coconut drops will keep stored in an airtight container for up to 3 days.

Turmeric coconut barfi

This adapted recipe uses dates with unsweetened oat milk to create a rich, sweet treat.

15 plump pitted/stoned dates

4 tablespoons unsweetened oat or soya/soy milk

4-cm/1½-inch piece of fresh turmeric, peeled, or use 1 teaspoon ground turmeric

1 tablespoon coconut oil

45 g/scant ½ cup blanched ground almonds

70 g/scant 1 cup desiccated/dried unsweetened shredded coconut, plus 1 tablespoon for sprinkling

1 scant teaspoon ground green cardamom seeds

20–25-cm/8–10-inch square baking pan, greased with extra-virgin coconut oil and base-lined with parchment

MAKES 16

Combine the dates, milk and turmeric root (if using powder, add later) in a food processor or blender and blitz until you have a smooth paste.

Add the coconut oil to a small heavy-bottomed pan and place over a medium–high heat. Once the oil is fully melted, add the date purée. Bring to a simmer, then reduce the heat to low and cook gently for 5–6 minutes; careful not to burn it.

Next, add the ground almonds, keeping the heat on low, and mix to form a soft dough. Then add the coconut and cardamom (and ground turmeric, if using). Remove from the heat, and mix until everything is evenly combined.

Press the mixture into the prepared baking pan, and spread the mixture evenly until it is smooth. Sprinkle the extra coconut on the top, pressing down lightly. Chill for 1 hour in the fridge.

Remove from the pan by running a knife around the edge and carefully tipping it out onto a board. Cut into diamond shapes, and store in an airtight container in the fridge for up to 1 week.

Maple choc nut fudge

The combination of tahini, cacao butter and macadamia nuts adds a creaminess to this dairy-free fudge.

60 g/2¼ oz. dark/bittersweet dairy-free chocolate, about 70% cocoa solids, broken into even-sized pieces

2 tablespoons tahini

25 g/1 oz. raw cacao butter

2 tablespoons maple syrup

100 g/3½ oz. sesame seeds

100 g/3½ oz. macadamia nuts

¼ teaspoon ground cinnamon

brownie pan, lined with cling film/plastic wrap, leaving enough overhang to cover the top

MAKES 24

Put the chocolate, tahini, cacao butter and maple syrup in a heatproof bowl. Place over a pan of simmering water (make sure the bottom of the bowl does not touch the water) and heat gently until everything is melted, giving the mixture an occasional stir. Leave to cool slightly.

Blitz the sesame seeds and macadamia nuts in a food processor or blender until they are finely chopped and turning buttery. Spoon the blended seeds and nuts into the chocolate mixture, add the cinnamon and stir until combined.

Spoon the chocolate mixture into the lined brownie pan and smooth with the back of a dampened spoon into an even layer, about 2 cm/¾ inch thick. Fold the overhanging cling film/plastic wrap over the top.

Freeze for 1 hour or until firm, then lift out of the pan using the cling film to help and cut into 24 2-cm/¾-inch squares. Store in the fridge in an airtight container for up to 2 weeks.

Couscous & jam crunchies

This is a great cookie with a crunchy texture and a really useful way to use up leftover store-cupboard essentials.

120 g/¾ cup couscous

160 g/1¾ cups ground almonds

130 g/1 cup unbleached plain/all-purpose flour

1 tablespoon ground flaxseeds

¼ teaspoon bourbon vanilla powder

¼ teaspoon sea salt

130 g/½ cup pure maple syrup

100 g/½ cup sunflower oil

½ teaspoon almond extract

200 g/⅔ cup plum or other thick, naturally sweetened jam/jelly

MAKES ABOUT 24

Preheat the oven to 180°C (350°F) Gas 4. Line 2 baking sheets with baking parchment.

Put the couscous, almonds, flour, flaxseeds, vanilla powder and salt in a mixing bowl and mix. Put the syrup, oil and almond extract in a separate bowl and whisk vigorously. Pour into the bowl of dry ingredients and mix with a wooden spoon.

Pull off walnut-sized pieces of dough and roll into balls. Flatten them between your palms until 1 cm/½ inch thick. Arrange them on the baking sheets spaced just slightly apart – they won't spread during baking.

Gently press a hole in the middle of each cookie – don't press too hard otherwise you might break through the bottom of the cookie. Fill each hole with a teaspoon of jam. Bake in the preheated oven for 15–16 minutes. Don't worry if they seem soft – they will harden as they cool down.

Remove from the oven and allow to cool on the baking sheets. Store in an airtight container for up to 2 weeks.

Summer berry muffins

A simple recipe for fruity, nutty muffins.

325 g/2½ cups plain/all-purpose flour

65 g/½ cup plain wholemeal/whole-wheat flour

1½ teaspoons bicarbonate of/baking soda

1 teaspoon baking powder

¼ teaspoon sea salt

65 g/1 cup ground hazelnuts

420 ml/1¾ cups plain soy milk

200 g/¾ cup brown rice syrup

150 g/¾ cup sunflower oil

freshly squeezed juice of ½ lemon

1 small apple, peeled, cored and chopped

48 raspberries (or a mix of berries)

12-hole muffin pan lined with paper cases

MAKES 12

Preheat the oven to 180°C (350°F) Gas 4.

Sift together the flours, bicarbonate of soda, baking powder and salt in a bowl and add the ground hazelnuts. Mix well.

Put the milk, syrup, oil, lemon juice and apple in a food processor and blend until smooth.

Combine the dry and liquid ingredients, and mix gently with a silicone spatula. Do not overmix otherwise the muffins will be tough.

Divide the cake mixture between the muffin cases. Gently press 4 raspberries into each muffin so that they are half-dipped in the mixture.

Bake in the preheated oven for 25–30 minutes. Allow to cool in the muffin pan for a few minutes, then transfer to a wire rack to cool completely.

Baked fruit & oat squares

These oaty squares are delicious served warm as dessert with vegan ice cream or coconut yogurt with extra maple syrup.

2 tablespoons ground chia seeds

190 g/2 cups rolled/old-fashioned oats

50 g/½ cup ground almonds

2 teaspoons ground cinnamon

1 teaspoon baking powder

¼ teaspoon sea salt

2 ripe bananas, roughly chopped

375 ml/1½ cups almond milk

60 ml/¼ cup pure maple syrup

3 tablespoons melted coconut oil

2 teaspoons pure vanilla extract

450 g/4–4½ cups strawberries, sliced

60 g/¾ cup flaked/sliced almonds

20-cm/8-inch square baking pan, greased with coconut oil

SERVES 7–9

Preheat the oven to 190°C (375°F) Gas 5.

In a medium bowl, make a 'chia egg' mixture by mixing the chia seeds with 6 tablespoons water. Let the mixture stand for 5 minutes.

In another bowl, combine the oats, ground almonds, cinnamon, baking powder and salt.

In the 'chia egg' bowl, mash the bananas with a fork. Add the milk, maple syrup, coconut oil and vanilla. Mix well to combine.

Add the dry ingredients to the wet ingredients and stir to combine. Add half of the sliced strawberries and 40 g/½ cup of the flaked almonds to the mixture, and pour everything evenly into the prepared baking pan.

Top with rows of the remaining strawberry slices and sprinkle the rest of the flaked almonds over the top. Bake in the oven for 35–40 minutes until set. Cut into portions. Store in an airtight container in the fridge for up to 5 days.

Paradise 'bounty' bars

Everyone needs a sweeter treat from time to time, and these little bars are the perfect tea break snack.

400-ml/14-oz. can coconut milk

100 g/1⅓ cups coarse desiccated/dried unsweetened shredded coconut, plus extra to decorate

50 g/¼ cup coconut yogurt

1 tablespoon date syrup, or use pure maple syrup

¼ teaspoon vanilla bean paste, or use ½ teaspoon vanilla extract

½ tablespoon extra-virgin coconut oil, melted

large pinch of sea salt

120 g/4 oz. vegan dark/bittersweet chocolate, at least 70% cocoa, broken into pieces

MAKES 8

Do not shake the can of coconut milk. Remove the can lid and, using a spoon, remove 120 ml/½ cup of the thickest part, leaving the watery part behind (you can use this for other dishes).

Place all the ingredients, except the chocolate, in a food processor and blitz until well combined and slightly smoother. Place the mixture onto a clean work surface, and shape into eight small bars. Place onto a baking sheet lined with baking parchment, cover and chill to set for at least 1 hour.

Place a small heatproof bowl over a small pan of simmering water. Add the chocolate to the bowl and let it melt gently. Carefully dip the bottom of the coconut bars into the chocolate, shaking to remove any excess, then place them back onto the baking sheet. Pour the remaining melted chocolate over the bars to create a smooth finish. Sprinkle each bar with a little extra coconut.

Return the coated bars to the fridge for another hour to set completely. The bars will keep in a covered container in the fridge for up to 1 week.

Index

RECIPE CREDITS

CAROLINE ARTISS
Chocolate and Avocado Balls

ROSS DOBSON
Spicy Cajun Mixed Nuts

URSULA FERRIGNO
Taralli

NICOLA GRAIMES
Banana Oat Bites
Beetroot and Ginger Balls
Cajun Tortilla Chips
Cauli 'Cheese' Bites
Coconut and Cherry Drops
Double Ginger Nut Bites
Dukkah Bean Balls
Grain-free 'Cheesy' Pumpkin
　Crackers
Japanese Rice Balls
Nori Miso Crisps
Power Green Bean Balls
Raspberry, Coconut and Lemon
　Bars
Savoury Granola Bar
Spiced Fruit Bars
Super Snack Balls
Sweet Potato and Quinoa Bites
Vegan Maple Choc Nut Fudge
Wasabi-roasted Edamame

DUNJA GULIN
Almond Butter Cups
Carob and Cocoa Fudge Bars
Cocoa Almond Freezer Fudge
　Pops
Coconut and Spirulina Balls
Coconut Cookies
Coffee Cookies
Couscous and Jam Crunchies

Ginger and Cashew Granola
　Bars
Summer Berry Muffins
Very Cherry Balls

VICKY JONES
Chickpea Fritters

JACKIE KEARNEY
Gourd and Cashew Koftas
Heart of Palm Calamari
Himalayan Energy Bars
Paradise 'Bounty' Bars
Turmeric Coconut Bari

ANYA LADRA
Brownie Bars
Salty Trail Mix

DAN MAY
Marinated Olives and Padron
　Peppers

HANNAH MILES
Thai Green Curry Popcorn

LOUISE PICKFORD
Breakfast Smoothie
Creamy Berry Soy Shake
Date and Banana Frappe
Soy and Tahini Smoothie

LEAH VANDERVELDT
Baked Strawberry, Banana and
　Oat Squares
Chickpea and Chocolate Chip
　Cookies
Chocolate Banana Bread
Green Smoothie Bowl
Oven-baked Rosemary Crisps
Topped Toasts
Ultimate Breakfast Sandwich

LAURA WASHBURN HUTTON
Aubergine and Sumac Fries

JENNA ZOE
Courgette Un-fries
Jalapeño Onion Rings
Creole Cauliflower
Spicy Tomato Kale Chips
Sports Bites
Tahini Protein Bites

PHOTOGRAPHY CREDITS

All photography by **CLAIRE
WINFIELD**, with the exception
of:

ED ANDERSON
Pages 26 bottom right, 29.

JAN BALDWIN
Page 65.

PETER CASSIDY
Pages 78 bottom right, 86.

TARA FISHER
Pages 56 top right, 66.

WILLIAM LINGWOOD
Pages 26 top right, 43, 56 top
left, 62.

STEVE PAINTER
Pages 7 top right, 95.

WILLIAM REAVELL
Pages 40, 56 bottom right, 61.

KATE WHITAKER
Pages 5, 7 top left, 30, 33, 58.